What Do You Like to Eat for Breakfast?

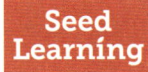
Seed Learning

What do you like to eat for breakfast?

I like to eat pancakes.

I like to eat pancakes for breakfast.

What do you like to eat for breakfast?

I like to eat waffles.

I like to eat waffles
for breakfast.

What do you like to eat for breakfast?

I like to eat omelets.

I like to eat omelets for breakfast.

What do you like to eat for breakfast?

I like to eat avocados.

I like to eat avocados
for breakfast.

What do you like to eat for breakfast?

I like to eat bacon.

I like to eat bacon
for breakfast.

What do you like to eat for breakfast?

I like to eat cereal.

I like to eat cereal
for breakfast.

What do you like to eat for breakfast?

I like to eat toast.

I like to eat toast
for breakfast.

Let's learn more about Mid-Autumn Festival.

Color the rabbit.